dump&bake

Dinners

One Dish.

Deliciously Easy.

Printed in the United States of America
by G&R Publishing Co.

Distributed By:

507 Industrial Street
Waverly, IA 50677

ISBN-13: 978-1-56383-539-1
Item #7125

One dish does it all!

Do things the easy way.

Unload the ingredients in your baking dish, slow cooker, or skillet.

Mix 'em up, spread 'em out, or simply layer – then cook as directed.

Prepare to be wowed by the delicious results!

Dump dinners are convenient one-dish meals. Since you're not browning, pre-cooking, or stirring things up in separate bowls, preparation and clean-up are quick and easy. And the flavor? Rich and satisfying. These tips make assembly even simpler:

✓ Save time by buying precut food, frozen or canned veggies, and fully cooked frozen meat crumbles.

✓ Buy extra canned items when they're on sale so you'll have them whenever you feel like making a quick dinner.

✓ Cut up fresh vegetables ahead of time *(how about right after you get home from the store?)* and refrigerate them in airtight containers so they're ready to use.

✓ For best results, fill your baking dishes no more than ¾ full. If you're worried about spill-overs, set the dish on a foil-lined rimmed baking sheet to catch drips.

✓ Many recipes can be made ahead and refrigerated for cooking in a day or two.

Simply Delicious.

Chicken Parmesan

½ onion, chopped

1 tsp. garlic powder

4 boneless skinless chicken cutlets

¼ C. panko bread crumbs

¼ C. shredded Parmesan cheese

¼ C. grated Parmesan cheese, divided

Paprika

3 or 4 plum tomatoes

2 each zucchini and yellow summer squash

2 or 3 small potatoes

1 T. olive oil

¾ tsp. Italian seasoning

Salt and black pepper

¼ C. shredded mozzarella cheese

preheat the oven to 375°. Grease an 11 x 13" baking dish.

spread onion in prepared dish and sprinkle with garlic powder. Place chicken in a single layer in the center and sprinkle evenly with bread crumbs, shredded Parmesan cheese, 2 tablespoons grated Parmesan, and a little paprika.

slice the tomatoes, zucchini, squash, and potatoes into ¼"- to ⅜"-thick rounds *(or cube them)* and arrange pieces around chicken as desired; drizzle with oil. Sprinkle Italian seasoning, salt, and pepper over everything.

cover and bake 35 to 40 minutes. Uncover and sprinkle vegetables with mozzarella cheese and remaining 2 tablespoons grated Parmesan. Bake 10 to 15 minutes more, until vegetables are tender and chicken is fully cooked. Set under a hot broiler briefly to brown the meat.

slow cooker
Teriyaki Chicken

½ C. teriyaki sauce

¼ C. soy sauce

½ C. brown sugar

1 T. sesame oil

1 tsp. finely shredded gingerroot

1 C. chicken broth

1½ tsp. minced garlic

2 lbs. boneless skinless chicken breasts, thinly sliced

3 large carrots, sliced into sticks

1 or 2 bell peppers (green, orange, and/or red), sliced

½ C. chopped onion

dump the teriyaki sauce, soy sauce, brown sugar, oil, gingerroot, broth, and garlic into an ungreased 3- or 4-quart slow cooker and stir to blend.

add the chicken, carrots, bell peppers, and onion; toss until coated.

cover and cook on low for 7 to 8 hours or on high about 4 hours, until everything is tender. (If you'd like to thicken the sauce at the end of the cooking time, remove about ½ cup of the hot liquid and stir in 2 heaping tablespoons cornstarch; pour the mixture back into the cooker and cook on high for 15 minutes until thickened.)

serve with hot cooked rice or chow mein noodles and sprinkle with sesame seed.

To add a little crunch, stir in a can of sliced water chestnuts (drained) before serving. Mmm....

chops &
Cornbread Stuffing

Preheat the oven to 400°. Grease a deep 9" pie plate. Place 4 *(¾" to 1" thick)* boneless pork chops in the pie plate and brush with 1 T. Dijon mustard; sprinkle each chop with a scant 1 tsp. brown sugar. Layer 1½ C. cornbread stuffing mix, 1 C. frozen *(thawed)* corn kernels, ½ C. chopped onion, and ¼ C. chopped celery over the chops. Season with salt and black pepper. Spread 1 (10.7 oz.) can cream of celery soup evenly over the top. Cover and bake for 45 minutes; uncover and bake 15 minutes longer, until chops are fully cooked.

Sweet Hawaiian Ham

Peel and cube three large sweet potatoes and dump into a deep 12" skillet. Core two large Jonagold apples and cut into ½"-thick rings; quarter them and add to the skillet. Cut a 1½ lb. ham steak into serving-size pieces and set the pieces on top; sprinkle with 1 tsp. cinnamon and ¼ C. brown sugar. Dump 1 (20 oz.) can pineapple chunks *(in heavy syrup)* over all, and toss on ¼ C. sliced butter. Sprinkle an additional 2 T. brown sugar over the top. Cover and cook on medium heat for 20 minutes; uncover and cook about 10 minutes more or until potatoes are tender. Let stand 5 to 10 minutes before serving.

drumsticks with Butternut Squash

1 medium butternut squash, peeled & cut into ¾" cubes

2 large Jonagold or Fuji apples, cored & cut into ¾" cubes

1 T. chopped fresh sage

¼ C. olive oil

Salt and black pepper

8 chicken legs (2½ to 3 lbs.)

Paprika

2 tsp. Montreal or other favorite chicken seasoning

3 T. butter, thinly sliced

preheat the oven to 400° F.

combine the squash, apples, and sage in an ungreased 9 x 13" baking dish or roasting pan. Drizzle with oil and season with salt and pepper; toss well.

arrange chicken legs over the squash combo and sprinkle them with salt, pepper, paprika, and chicken seasoning. Dot the drumsticks evenly with butter slices.

bake uncovered for 1 hour 10 minutes or until chicken is golden brown and cooked through and squash is tender.

Oven Omelet

Preheat the oven to 375°. Lightly grease a deep 9″ casserole dish. Crack 9 eggs into prepared dish and whisk well. Then whisk in ½ C. milk. Add 1 C. diced ham, 1 chopped and seeded tomato, 3 T. finely chopped onion, 2 T. minced fresh parsley, and ¼ tsp. each black pepper and red pepper flakes; mix well. Stir in 1 C. shredded Swiss cheese and ½ C. shredded cheddar cheese. Cover with foil and bake 40 to 45 minutes or until set and a knife inserted in the center comes out clean. Remove foil and bake uncovered about 5 minutes more to brown lightly.

Pepperoni Ravioli

Preheat the oven to 350°. In an ungreased 2-quart baking dish, combine 1 (25 oz.) pkg. frozen beef or cheese ravioli *(thawed)*, 1 (4 oz.) can sliced mushrooms *(drained)*, 1 sliced medium zucchini, ½ C. pepperoni slices, and 1 (24 oz.) jar roasted tomato & garlic pasta sauce; toss until well coated. Sprinkle with 1 to 2 C. shredded provolone cheese, ¼ tsp. Italian seasoning, and ½ tsp. dried basil. Bake uncovered for 40 to 50 minutes or until hot and bubbly.

slow cooker
Meatloaf Dinner

1 egg

¼ C. milk

2 bread slices, crumbled

1½ tsp. salt

Black pepper

1½ lbs. 90% to 95% lean ground beef

½ C. chopped onion

2 T. green bell pepper, diced

1 celery rib, diced

Ketchup to taste

6 medium potatoes, halved

2 T. butter, melted

Seasoned salt

crack the egg into a lightly greased 4- to 6-quart slow cooker and beat lightly.

add milk, crumbled bread, salt, and pepper to taste; stir and let stand about 5 minutes. Add beef, onion, bell pepper, and celery; mix well.

shape mixture into a loaf and spread ketchup over the top as desired. Arrange potatoes next to the loaf; drizzle butter over potatoes and toss lightly. Sprinkle with seasoned salt.

cover and cook on high for 2 hours; then reduce heat to low and cook 2½ to 3 hours longer, until meatloaf is cooked through and potatoes are tender.

Mix it up in your slow cooker for dump & bake ease.

Chicken *easy* Pot Pie

2 (12.5 oz.) cans white meat chicken

2 (10.5 oz.) cans cream of chicken soup

2 (14.5 oz.) cans sliced carrots, drained

2 (15 oz.) cans diced potatoes, drained

2 C. frozen petite peas

Salt and black pepper

1 (8 oz.) tube crescent seamless dough sheet

Cooking spray

Coarse salt

preheat the oven to 350°.

dump both cans of chicken *(including the juice)* into an ungreased 9 x 13" baking dish and shred lightly with a fork. Stir in both cans of soup and all the vegetables until combined. Season with salt and pepper and spread evenly in dish.

unroll the dough sheet and flatten into a 9 x 13" rectangle. Set the dough over the ingredients in dish, covering completely. Spritz dough with cooking spray and sprinkle lightly with coarse salt.

bake uncovered for 40 to 50 minutes or until top crust is golden brown and filling is bubbly.

Fiesta Chicken

1 C. uncooked long-grain white rice

1 C. frozen corn kernels, thawed

1 (15 oz.) can black beans, drained & rinsed

1 (16 oz.) jar salsa

1 C. chicken broth

1½ to 2 tsp. chili powder

½ tsp. dried oregano

Salt and black pepper

1½ lbs. boneless skinless chicken breasts, cut into strips

1 C. shredded Mexican cheese blend

Chopped tomatoes

preheat the oven to 375° and lightly grease a 9 x 9" baking dish.

combine the rice, corn, beans, salsa, broth, chili powder, and oregano in prepared dish; season with salt and pepper and stir gently until well mixed.

press the chicken strips down into the rice mixture in dish until covered.

cover with foil and bake 1½ to 1¾ hours or until rice is tender and chicken is cooked through. Uncover and sprinkle cheese over the top; cover again and let stand about 5 minutes to melt the cheese. Sprinkle with tomatoes before serving.

Meatball Sub Bake

Preheat the oven to 350°. Open 1 (16.3 oz.) tube refrigerated "grands" biscuits and cut each biscuit into six equal pieces. Scatter them in an ungreased 9 x 13" baking dish. Layer with 1 (16 oz.) pkg. frozen cooked Italian meatballs *(or homemade)* and 1 diced green bell pepper. Pour 1 (24 oz.) jar pasta sauce over the top and sprinkle with 2 C. shredded Italian 5-cheese blend. Bake for 45 to 55 minutes or until biscuits are done and cheese is melted and golden brown. Before serving, sprinkle with Parmesan cheese and chopped chives, if you'd like.

creamy
Chicken Hot Potatoes

Cut 2 lbs. boneless skinless chicken breasts into large strips.
In a greased 6-quart slow cooker, combine chicken and
2 (8 oz.) pkgs. cream cheese *(cubed)*. Sprinkle 2 (1 oz.) packets
dry ranch dressing mix over the top and stir well; cover the
mixture with parchment paper. Pierce 5 scrubbed baking
potatoes with a knife and wrap in foil; set potatoes on the
parchment paper. Cover slow cooker and cook on high
5 hours or until potatoes are done. Remove potatoes and
discard parchment paper. Shred the meat in the cooker, add
5 chopped precooked bacon strips, and stir to combine all
ingredients. Unwrap the potatoes and cut as desired; top with
hot chicken mixture, shredded cheese, parsley, and more
bacon. *(This chicken also tastes great on sandwich buns.)*

Simple Tex-Mex Quinoa

1½ lbs. butternut squash, peeled, seeded & cubed

1¼ C. frozen corn kernels

1 (15 oz.) can black beans, drained & rinsed

1 C. uncooked quinoa, rinsed & drained

1 tsp. minced garlic

1 (14.5 oz.) can fire-roasted diced tomatoes

1 jalapeño pepper, seeded & diced

2 (10 oz.) cans red enchilada sauce *(we used 1 hot and 1 mild)*

1 C. vegetable broth

1 (1.25 oz.) packet taco seasoning

Salt and black pepper

Crispy tortilla salad shells, optional

grease a 5-quart slow cooker.

dump the squash, corn, beans, rinsed quinoa, garlic, tomatoes *(with liquid)*, jalapeño, enchilada sauce, broth, and taco seasoning into the cooker and stir until well combined.

cover and cook on high for 3½ to 4 hours or until quinoa is cooked and squash is almost tender. Uncover and stir. Reduce heat to low and cook about 30 minutes more, until liquid is mostly absorbed. Season with salt and pepper.

serve in salad shells, if you'd like, and top with a squeeze of lime juice, some chopped tomatoes, shredded cheese, sour cream, and/or fresh cilantro. Olé!

Lemon-Garlic
Salmon Bake

4 (4 oz.) skinless
  salmon fillets

10 to 12 oz. frozen whole
  green beans, thawed
  but still cold

1 pt. cherry tomatoes
  (about 20)

Olive oil

Salt and black pepper

Lemon-Garlic Butter
  (recipe follows)

preheat the oven to 400°. Grease a 9 x 13" baking dish.

arrange the salmon fillets in the center of prepared dish. Place green beans and tomatoes on each side of the salmon.

drizzle a little oil over the vegetables and season them with salt and pepper. Spread some of the Lemon-Garlic Butter yumminess over each fillet.

bake uncovered for 20 to 22 minutes or until salmon flakes with a fork and green beans are crisp-tender. If you'd like, spritz the beans with cooking spray after 15 minutes of baking to keep them moist and shiny.

Lemon-Garlic Butter

Stir together ¼ C. soft butter, 1 tsp. lemon zest, 1 T. lemon juice, 2 tsp. finely chopped fresh parsley, 2 tsp. finely chopped fresh thyme (or rosemary), 1 clove minced garlic, ¼ tsp. salt, and ¼ tsp. black pepper until well blended. (Make a larger batch and refrigerate for use with other seafood dishes.)

ham & Hashbrown Bake

1 (8 oz.) container
  sour cream

1 (5.3 oz.) container plain
  nonfat Greek yogurt

1 (10.7 oz.) can cream
  of celery soup

¼ C. chopped onion

1 (32 oz.) pkg. frozen
  diced hash browns

1 (12 oz.) pkg. diced ham
  (about 2 C.)

2 C. cubed American cheese

2 C. crushed corn flakes

½ C. butter, melted

preheat the oven to 350°.

dump the sour cream, yogurt, soup, and onion in an ungreased 9 x 13" baking dish and stir until blended.

fold in the hash browns, ham, and cheese. Spread evenly and scatter corn flakes over the top; drizzle with butter.

bake uncovered for 55 to 60 minutes or until golden brown on top and cooked through.

For a change, try other crunchy toppings in place of the corn flakes, like crushed potato chips or croutons.

wild rice
Pork Chops

Preheat the oven to 350°. Rinse 1½ C. wild/brown rice blend with hot water; drain well and spread in a greased 11 x 13" baking dish. Scatter 1 C. chopped carrot, ¾ C. chopped onion, and 2 (8 oz.) cans drained sliced mushrooms evenly over rice. Slowly pour in 2¼ C. hot water and sprinkle with 1½ T. chicken bouillon granules. Sprinkle both sides of five or six (¾" thick) bone-in pork chops with seasoned salt and black pepper. Arrange the chops on top of rice mixture and spread 1½ to 2 (10.7 oz.) cans cream of mushroom soup over everything. Cover with foil and bake for 2 hours or until rice is done and chops are tender. Uncover, increase oven temperature to 400°, and continue to bake 10 to 15 minutes more to lightly brown the meat. Stir the rice mixture before serving with chops.

Toss & Turn Stromboli

Preheat the oven to 400°. Unroll 1 (13.8 oz.) tube refrigerated pizza crust dough on a large parchment paper-lined cookie sheet and flatten into a 12 x 14" rectangle. Layer 12 oz. thinly sliced honey ham and 12 thin slices hard salami over the dough, leaving 1" uncovered along edges. Spread ⅓ C. ranch dressing over meat and sprinkle with 1½ C. shredded white cheddar cheese. Toss on 1 C. chopped tomatoes. Brush dough edges with egg substitute, and starting from one long edge, roll the dough into a log. Pinch all edges to seal filling inside. Turn the log seam side down on the parchment paper and brush the top with egg substitute. Sprinkle with coarse black pepper, garlic salt, and grated Parmesan cheese. Bake 30 to 35 minutes or until golden brown and bubbly. Let rest 10 minutes before slicing.

Lazy Day Beef Stew

2 lbs. beef stew meat

3 medium potatoes, peeled

5 medium carrots, peeled

1 onion

2 C. frozen cut green beans

⅓ C. water

½ tsp. salt, or more to taste

½ tsp. black pepper, or more to taste

1 (10.7 oz.) can tomato soup

1 (10.7 oz.) can cream of mushroom soup

preheat the oven to 275° and generously grease a deep 9 x 13" baking dish.

cut the beef, potatoes, carrots, and onion into 1" chunks and add to prepared dish. Add the green beans and water. Season with salt and pepper and toss together well.

pour the tomato and mushroom soups over the top and stir lightly to combine.

cover with foil and bake 4 to 5 hours, until everything is nice and tender *(no thickening needed)*.

Kick the flavor up a notch...

Add any of the following: 1 C. sliced celery, a splash or two of red wine or Worcestershire sauce, some seasoned salt or cayenne pepper, or a small packet of beef stew mix or dry onion soup mix.

serves 6-8

So Simple Skillet Lasagna

Grease a deep 12" skillet and spread ½ (9.6 oz.) pkg. fully cooked sausage crumbles *(like Jimmy Dean brand)* over the bottom. Layer with ¼ C. chopped onion and ¾ C. sliced fresh mushrooms; season with garlic salt and black pepper. Cover with a layer of uncooked lasagna noodles, breaking them to fit *(use about four)*. Spread ½ (24 oz.) jar pasta sauce over noodles and top with ½ (10 oz.) can diced tomatoes with chiles *(undrained)* and ½ C. water. Repeat to make a second layer. Bring to a full simmer over medium-high heat; reduce heat to medium-low, cover the pan, and simmer 30 to 35 minutes, until noodles are tender. Uncover and drop ¾ C. ricotta cheese over the top by spoonfuls. Sprinkle with 1 C. shredded mozzarella cheese and ⅓ C. shredded Parmesan. Cover and cook 5 minutes more.

Chic-quick-n- Veggie Quiche

Preheat the oven to 400°. Thaw and drain 1 C. frozen chopped onion and 1 (10 oz.) pkg. frozen chopped spinach. Dump 1 (6 oz.) pkg. stuffing mix for chicken into a greased 9 x 9" baking dish. Stir in 1½ C. boiling water and ¼ C. egg substitute; press mixture into bottom of dish. Layer with ¾ C. shredded cheddar & Monterey Jack cheese blend, half the onions, half the spinach, and 1½ C. shredded rotisserie chicken; sprinkle with salt and black pepper. Slice ½ red bell pepper and place over the top. Repeat the layers of cheese, onions, spinach, chicken, salt, and pepper. Pour 1 C. egg substitute evenly over all and arrange tomato slices on top. Bake 40 to 45 minutes or until bubbly around the edges. Let stand 10 minutes before cutting.

serves 8

sweet raspberry Chipotle Pork

2 T. canola oil

1 T. minced garlic

1 tsp. onion powder

1 T. dried minced onion

2½ tsp. salt, divided

½ tsp. black pepper, divided

1 (16 oz.) jar roasted raspberry chipotle salsa, divided

1 (3 lb.) pork loin roast

4 large sweet potatoes, peeled & chopped into ½" to ¾" chunks

1 onion, cut into chunks

preheat the oven to 350°. Grease a 9 x 13" baking dish.

combine the oil, garlic, onion powder, dried minced onion, 1½ teaspoons salt, ¼ teaspoon pepper, and ½ cup salsa in prepared pan; stir well and spread evenly. Add the pork roast and turn to coat.

place the sweet potatoes and onion around the meat and sprinkle vegetables with the remaining 1 teaspoon salt and ¼ teaspoon pepper.

cover and bake 1 hour or until the meat registers 145° on a meat thermometer and the sweet potatoes are tender. Let stand 10 minutes before slicing meat. Serve with the remaining salsa.

Want more veggies? Try adding about 1¼ lbs. Brussels sprouts to the pan along with the sweet potatoes and onions.

unstuffed Cabbage Rolls

Preheat the oven to 400°. Cut one head green cabbage into bite-size pieces and toss half into a greased 9 x 13" baking dish. Crumble 1 lb. raw lean ground beef over the cabbage and season with salt and black pepper. Layer on 1 chopped onion, 1½ C. uncooked Arborio or other short-grain rice, and 2 (14.5 oz.) cans diced tomatoes with basil, garlic & oregano. Sprinkle with more salt and pepper. Put the remaining cabbage on top. Spread 1 (10.7 oz.) can tomato soup evenly over the cabbage and slowly pour one soup can of water over all. Cover with foil and bake for 1½ hours. Let stand 10 minutes. Sprinkle with shredded Parmesan cheese and sliced green onions before serving.

skillet sausage
Penne & vegetables

Cut 13 to 16 oz. smoked sausage into ¼"-thick slices.
Pour 1 T. olive oil into a deep 10" skillet over medium-high
heat. Add the sausage, ½ C. chopped onion, 1 (12 oz.) pkg.
frozen mixed vegetables *(we used the steamable type with
asparagus, corn & carrots)*, 2½ C. chicken broth, ½ C. milk,
and 8 oz. uncooked penne pasta. Stir until well combined.
Cover and bring to a boil and then reduce the heat to
medium to maintain a boil. Cook for 12 minutes; uncover
and cook 3 minutes longer or until pasta is done to your
liking. Season with salt, black pepper, and garlic powder to
taste. Turn off the heat and let stand a few minutes to thicken
slightly. Sprinkle with ½ C. grated Parmesan cheese
before serving.

loaded
Baked Potato Dish

4½ C. washed & diced russet or red potatoes, divided

1 lb. boneless skinless chicken breasts, diced

¾ tsp. salt, divided

½ tsp. black pepper, divided

4 precooked bacon slices, crumbled, divided

1½ C. shredded cheddar cheese, divided

3 to 4 green onions, sliced, divided

½ C. heavy cream

2 T. butter, sliced

Sour cream

preheat the oven to 350°. Grease a 9 x 9" baking dish.

spread half the potatoes in prepared dish. Scatter chicken pieces over the potatoes and sprinkle with ½ teaspoon salt and ¼ teaspoon pepper. Top with half the bacon, ½ cup cheese, and half the green onions.

layer with the remaining potatoes and bacon, ½ cup cheese, remaining green onions, and remaining ¼ teaspoon each salt and pepper. Pour cream over the top and dot with butter slices.

cover with foil and bake 1 hour. Uncover and bake 30 minutes more. Sprinkle the remaining ½ cup cheese over the top and let set a few minutes to melt. Top with sour cream and any of your favorite baked potato toppings.

For a rich smoky flavor, try smoked cheddar cheese in this dish.

Cajun Combo

3 lbs. skinless bone-in chicken pieces *(we used thighs)*

2 (19 oz.) pkgs. sweet Italian sausage links, thawed & cut into chunks

Salt and black pepper

Cajun seasoning

2 lbs. white new potatoes, washed & quartered

2 green bell peppers, cut into chunks

2 onions, cut into chunks

2 celery ribs, cut into chunks

¼ C. vegetable oil

preheat the oven to 350°.

combine the chicken and sausage pieces in a deep ungreased 9 x 13" baking dish or roasting pan. Sprinkle with salt, pepper, and a hefty dose of Cajun seasoning to taste.

add the potatoes, bell peppers, onions, and celery. Drizzle oil over the top and toss vegetables until coated. Add more salt, pepper, and Cajun seasoning and toss again.

cover with foil and bake 2½ to 3 hours or until chicken and sausage are done and vegetables are tender.

Serve this dish with cornbread and finish off your meal with beignets as a salute to New Orleans.

foil pack
Seafood Combo

Preheat the oven to 400°. Layer 2 (18") squares of heavy-duty foil on a cookie sheet. Arrange 1 lb. sliced fingerling potatoes in the center and set 4 (4 to 5 oz.) cod filets in a single layer on top. Dot fish with 2 T. sliced butter. Sprinkle with garlic powder, salt, black pepper, and chopped fresh dill. Add 8 oz. frozen raw shrimp *(thawed, peeled & deveined)* and 8 oz. scallops *(thawed)* on top, followed by a few lemon slices and a handful of grape tomatoes. Place 4 (2") chunks of sweet corn beside the food and set ½ T. butter on each chunk. Sprinkle with more garlic powder, salt, pepper, and dill. Wrap foil around food, crimping edges tightly to seal. Bake 45 minutes or until seafood is cooked through and potatoes are tender.

Robust Reuben Bake

Preheat the oven to 400°. Set aside 8 slices from a 1 lb. party loaf of rye or pumpernickel bread. Tear up 40 more slices and arrange pieces evenly in a greased 9 x 13" baking dish. Spread 1 (14 oz.) can drained sauerkraut over the bread in dish. Cut 1 lb. deli-sliced corned beef into strips and layer them over the sauerkraut. Drizzle with ¾ C. to 1 C. Thousand Island dressing; sprinkle lightly with caraway seed, if you'd like. Cut the set-aside bread slices in half diagonally to make 16 triangles; spritz with cooking spray and arrange them around edge of dish, setting any extras on top. Cover with foil and bake 25 to 30 minutes. Remove foil and sprinkle with 2 C. shredded Swiss cheese. Bake uncovered about 10 minutes longer or until cheese melts and everything is bubbly. Serve with more dressing.

Southwestern Chicken Casserole

1 (12 oz.) can evaporated milk

1 (10.75 oz.) can cheddar cheese soup

½ C. salsa

¼ tsp. black pepper

2 tsp. seasoned salt

1 (14 to 16 oz.) pkg. frozen southwest-style or fiesta vegetable blend, thawed*

2 C. chopped rotisserie chicken

1½ C. uncooked instant white rice

1 C. shredded Mexican cheese blend

½ C. sour cream

Our blend contained broccoli, corn, carrots, kidney beans, garbanzos, Italian green beans, and red peppers.

preheat the oven to 350°. Grease a 9 x 13" baking dish.

pour evaporated milk and soup into prepared dish and whisk together well. Add salsa, pepper, seasoned salt, vegetables, chicken, and rice; stir until combined.

cover with foil and bake about 35 minutes.

uncover and sprinkle with cheese. Bake 10 to 15 minutes longer or until cheese melts and everything is hot and bubbly. Let stand about 5 minutes. Top with sour cream before serving.

3-Meat Skillet Pizza

1 (9.6 oz.) pkg. frozen fully cooked sausage crumbles, thawed

1 (3.5 oz.) pkg. Canadian bacon, chopped *(about 35 slices)*

½ C. mini pepperoni, divided

1 (24 oz.) jar pasta sauce

2 C. water

2 tsp. dried oregano

½ tsp. garlic salt

Black pepper

8 oz. uncooked rotini pasta *(about 2⅔ C.)*

Diced bell pepper, sliced black olives, and sliced mushrooms, optional

1 to 2 C. shredded mozzarella cheese

Grated Parmesan cheese, optional

combine the sausage crumbles, Canadian bacon, and ¼ cup pepperoni in an ungreased 12" oven-safe skillet; place over medium heat and cook 1 to 2 minutes, just until warmed.

add the pasta sauce, water, oregano, garlic salt, pepper, and pasta; stir to combine. Fold in some bell pepper, black olives, and/or mushrooms, if you'd like.

bring the mixture to a boil. Cover the skillet, reduce heat to medium-low, and simmer 14 to 18 minutes or until pasta is tender and most of the liquid is absorbed. Meanwhile, preheat the oven's broiler.

remove skillet from heat. Sprinkle mozzarella cheese and remaining ¼ cup pepperoni over the pasta and place under the broiler for 1 to 2 minutes, until cheese is melted and lightly browned. Sprinkle with Parmesan cheese before serving, if you'd like.

Try using sausage-flavored pasta sauce, shaved Parmesan, and fresh mozzarella, then sprinkle chopped fresh basil over the top before serving. Delizioso!

Slow 'n' Cheesy Potatoes

Dump 1 (10.5 oz.) can cream of chicken with herbs soup
and 1 C. sour cream into a lightly greased 3- to 4-quart slow
cooker. Add 1½ C. shredded smoked cheddar cheese,
1 (24 oz.) pkg. frozen shredded hash browns with onion
& peppers *(thawed)*, and 3 C. diced turkey to cooker; stir
everything together. Cover and cook on low about 6 hours
or until hot and bubbly. Before serving, top with crushed
croutons *(try cheese & garlic-flavored)*.

Quick Noodle Bowl

In a medium saucepan, stir together the flavor packet
from 1 (3 oz.) pkg. Oriental-flavored ramen noodle soup,
2 C. water, 1 C. chopped green onions, and 2 T. chopped fresh
cilantro. Set pan over medium heat and add the noodles,
1 C. trimmed fresh snow peas, and 12 raw medium shrimp
(thawed, peeled & deveined). Bring to a simmer and cook
about 3 minutes or until noodles are tender and shrimp
are pink. Season with garlic salt, black pepper, and a dash
of cayenne pepper, if you'd like. Divide among bowls and
top with some shredded napa cabbage, more cilantro, and
chopped peanuts before serving.

serves 4

Chicken-Veggie Bake

4 boneless skinless chicken breast halves

1 lb. red potatoes, halved or quartered

½ yellow or red bell pepper, thinly sliced

½ onion, thinly sliced

2 C. fresh broccoli florets

1 (8 oz.) pkg. fresh white mushrooms, cleaned

1 yellow summer squash, thickly sliced

Salt and black pepper

½ C. butter, melted

1 (.7 oz.) packet dry Italian dressing mix

preheat the oven to 350°.

arrange chicken pieces in the center of an ungreased 9 x 13" baking dish. Dump the potatoes, bell pepper, onion, broccoli, mushrooms, and squash around chicken, combining them as desired. Season everything with salt and pepper.

drizzle butter over all and sprinkle evenly with dressing mix.

cover with foil and bake about 50 minutes or until chicken is done and potatoes are tender.

Dirty Rice

1 (10.7 oz.) can cream of celery soup

1 (10.5 oz.) can French onion soup

1 C. uncooked instant white rice

½ C. chopped green bell pepper

½ C. chopped celery

½ C. sliced green onions

1 tsp. salt

½ to 1 tsp. cayenne pepper, or to taste

1 lb. ground sausage

Coarse black pepper

Cajun seasoning

preheat the oven to 425°. Lightly grease a 2-quart casserole dish.

dump both soups into prepared dish and stir together. Add the rice, bell pepper, celery, green onions, salt, and cayenne pepper; stir until well combined.

crumble the raw sausage over ingredients in dish and fold into the rice mixture. Spread evenly and sprinkle with black pepper and Cajun seasoning as desired. Cover tightly with a double layer of foil.

bake about 1 hour or until meat is thoroughly cooked and rice is tender.

Use this dirty rice mixture as a filling for Cajun-style lettuce wraps or tacos, too.

corned Beef & Cabbage

1 (2½ to 3 lb.) corned beef brisket

1 T. flour

½ tsp. ground allspice

½ tsp. salt

½ tsp. black pepper

1 head green cabbage, cored

1 onion

3 large carrots, peeled

½ C. water

preheat the oven to 350°. Grease a 9 x 13" baking dish.

coat both sides of the brisket with flour and place in prepared dish. Sprinkle meat with allspice, salt, and pepper.

slice the cabbage into six wedges. Slice the onion into rings and the carrots into sticks. Arrange the vegetables around the meat and add the water.

cover with foil and bake about 2 hours or until the meat registers 175° with a meat thermometer and is fork-tender. Let stand 10 minutes before slicing.

Easy Shepherd's Pie

1 (15 oz.) pkg. refrigerated
  beef tips & gravy *(like
  Hormel brand)*

2 (15 oz.) cans mixed
  vegetables, drained

1 T. dried minced onion

½ tsp. dried minced garlic

½ tsp. beef bouillon
  granules

1 T. ketchup

Salt and black pepper

2 (21 oz.) containers
  refrigerated ready-to-use
  mashed potatoes,
  any flavor

Paprika

preheat the oven to 350°. Grease a 9 x 9" baking dish.

dump the beef and gravy into prepared dish and add
the mixed vegetables, onion, garlic, bouillon granules, and
ketchup. Season with salt and pepper and stir to combine.

spread mashed potatoes over the top and sprinkle
with paprika.

bake for 25 minutes or until heated through. To brown the
potatoes a bit after baking, place the dish under a hot broiler
just until desired crispiness and browning is achieved.

*If the potatoes are too stiff to spread, stir them or
microwave briefly before using. (You may substitute
about 5 cups leftover mashed potatoes for the
packaged variety, if you prefer.)*

firecracker
Shrimp Pack

Preheat the oven to 450°. Cut a large piece of heavy-duty foil, lay it on a rimmed baking sheet, and coat with cooking spray. Thaw 1 (12 oz.) pkg. frozen, cooked, and peeled shrimp *(tails removed)*; drain well and toss it off-center on the foil. Partially thaw 1 (10 oz.) pkg. frozen steamable rice & vegetable blend and dump it onto the foil next to the shrimp. Sprinkle with ½ tsp. garlic powder and season to taste with salt, black pepper, and crushed red pepper flakes. Pour ¾ C. chunky salsa down the middle. Fold foil around the food in a tent pack, sealing well, and bake 20 to 30 minutes or until shrimp are fully cooked and rice is hot. Carefully open the pack and drizzle a little lime juice over the food before serving.

cheesy
Sausage Tortellini

Preheat the oven to 400°. Grease a 9 x 13" baking dish.
Pour 1½ C. water and 1 (24 oz.) jar of your favorite pasta
sauce into prepared dish and stir to blend. Add 1 C. shredded
mozzarella cheese, 2 (8 oz.) pkgs. fully cooked sausage &
bacon crumbles *(we used Jimmy Dean brand)*, 2 T. shredded
Parmesan cheese, and 1 (19 oz.) bag frozen cheese tortellini.
Gently stir together to coat everything. Cover with foil and
bake for 35 minutes. Remove foil and top with another cup
of shredded mozzarella and some Parmesan cheese. Bake
5 to 10 minutes more, until cheese melts and dish is bubbly.

mexican Tortilla Stack

- 1 T. butter, softened
- 1⅓ C. refried beans
- 4 (8") flour tortillas, divided
- 1 T. taco seasoning mix, divided
- 1½ C. frozen veggie crumbles *(like Morning Star brand)*, thawed, divided
- 1 (10 oz.) can diced tomatoes with green chiles, drained, divided

- ⅔ C. chopped bell pepper, any color, divided
- ⅔ C. sliced green onions, divided
- 1 C. frozen corn kernels, thawed, divided
- ⅔ C. salsa, divided
- 2½ C. shredded Mexican cheese blend, divided

Sliced black olives

Fresh cilantro

preheat the oven to 400°. Butter the bottom of a deep 9" pie plate.

spread ⅓ cup refried beans over one side of each tortilla, almost to the edge. Set one tortilla in prepared pie plate, bean side up, and sprinkle evenly with 1 teaspoon taco seasoning. Layer with ½ cup veggie crumbles and ⅓ each of the tomatoes, bell pepper, green onions, and corn. Top with 3 to 4 tablespoons salsa and ½ cup cheese. Repeat to make two more complete layers starting with the prepped tortillas and pressing down slightly on each layer to make them level.

set the remaining tortilla on top and cover with remaining 1 cup cheese.

cover with greased foil and bake 30 minutes or until heated through. Uncover and let stand 5 to 10 minutes. Sprinkle with black olives and cilantro. Slice in wedges and serve with shredded lettuce, tomatoes, jalapeños, and sour cream as desired.

Just spread, sprinkle, stack, and bake to get layers of deliciousness!

one pot
Parmesan Spaghetti

1 (16 oz.) pkg. uncooked spaghetti, broken in half

1 (13.5 oz.) pkg. smoked Andouille sausage, thinly sliced

1 onion, thinly sliced

3 C. halved grape tomatoes

2 C. fresh basil leaves, loosely packed

2 tsp. minced garlic

5 C. water

Salt and black pepper

½ to 1 C. grated Parmesan cheese

combine the spaghetti, sausage, onion, tomatoes, basil, garlic, and water in a large Dutch oven or stockpot over medium heat. Season with salt and pepper and stir well.

bring the mixture to a boil; reduce heat and simmer uncovered for 10 to 15 minutes or until pasta is tender and liquid is reduced.

stir in Parmesan cheese and serve promptly.

Index